THE CHRISTMAS PRAYER

CATRINA McDERMOTT

Through faith and love,
And to that special someone
Happy Christmas!

Author Introduction

I am a teacher from County Fermanagh in Northern Ireland. I have always had a passion for writing; creating a world that expands and engages the mind, bringing the reader to a place where they can also relate to the story and absorb the hope and fun in doing so. I write both adult and children fiction stories, and others based on experience and non-fiction events.

SYNOPSIS

This is a heart-warming story about a young girl who becomes incredibly sad on Christmas Day. She is a girl who is hurting whilst she sits amongst her family, not fully understanding why. Then it hits her, and the little girl realises what she is missing. As the celebrations become too much for her, she leaves the cheers and the fun behind to find a quiet space – a peace of her own – where she says a little prayer to a nativity scene that lights up the whole room. She asks a favour from the baby Jesus, lying so still in his wooden crib.

Years later, when she is grown up, she is sitting alone on a train, although, not really alone at all. She is writing stories for kids, when suddenly she is interrupted and becomes distracted. She soon remembers her Christmas prayer, as she finally gets what she asked for so many years ago when she was just a child.

THE CHRISTMAS PRAYER

SNOWFLAKES gently fell upon the ground outside; everything was so quiet, everything so white. There was the perfect chill, the perfect scene, as the weak snowflake showed off its dominance, both in the air and on the ground. The peace encouraged stillness, as the birds ducked for cover. Nature's present had come to fill us with joy, so simple and so nice. Gorgeous! Glorious! Miraculous!

Inside the house, on this Christmas Day, it was

not quite the same, not so simple, and not so nice. Amidst the laughter and the celebrations, a sad, little girl sat at the table with her family, suffering in silence, as the clock continued to sound, again and again; tick-tock, tick-tock, tick-tock.

Although the little girl loved Christmas and everything about it, her heart ached, and she wasn't quite sure why. There was a thickness in her throat that lingered, causing her relentless pain. As she looked at the beauty that was all around her, the glow that came with this special day, she wondered why it was not making her happy – as it had so many times before.

Christmas was her favourite time of the year, giving her much excitement and energy, and she was always at the ready to count it down again, just as soon as it was over. She was the definition of Christmas and as jolly as the occasion. An everlasting buzz would always light up her heart, giving her that warm, lifted feeling, something she would quickly spread to others; the perfect influence.

There was always plenty to be psyched about,

as the little girl would enjoy every moment, every gift. She would absorb every experience, every memory: the food, the fun, the lights, the tree, and the togetherness. She had loved it all! But not today! Not this Christmas! Something was holding her back; something had switched her off from her beloved Christmas!

The little girl was in pain and struggled to hide it. There was a huge emptiness inside her, a feeling of being incomplete, like she was missing something, and because of this, the little girl was hurting. Her heart was breaking. She was a shy, little girl, who did not want anybody to see her cry. Suddenly, she was taken in by it all, distracted by the overexcited joke tellers, and the laughter that followed.

Stressful as it was to hide her unhappiness, she was relieved when they laughed, as it let her know when to laugh too; a fake act that helped her to blend in with them, hiding her sadness even more.

As she tried to chew and swallow the turkey, she

could feel it coming, and she could not stop it. It was like vomit. Out of her control! That lump again! Bigger and stronger than before! The curse that closed her throat and made it sore. The pain that was throwing her feelings to the surface, like pollen meeting the spring air, or the force of the chill on a cold winter's night, was impossible to ignore. Nothing was going to help it! Nothing was going to stop it! It was coming fast, as was the panic. *I hope nobody is looking*, she thought, as she tried to cling onto her straight face a little longer.

Her gaze set upon her family once more, and all of a sudden, the young girl developed a wish – a wish that, until now, she never knew she needed. As she watched her siblings so happy, she realised she needed something they had, something she was missing.

She needed a friend, a person that could love and care for her too, someone she could share and have fun with, a person who would be there for her, that would provide never-ending love and support; a soulmate.

Her heart continued to break, as she looked at

the scene playing out in front of her. Although she was happy for her siblings, she could not help but be a little envious, jealous even, as she was forced to watch everybody else so happy; a normality that she did not have, a sense of belonging that she did not feel.

Instead, more than ever before, a big, empty space started to reveal itself within her life. It was a hole that needed to be filled, a hunger and thirst for somebody; the cure for loneliness. The little girl glanced at her family before becoming lost in her thoughts once more, the background noise drowning itself out as she did. Her body was present in the middle of it all, but her mind was elsewhere.

How amazing would it be, to have someone to care for me like that, for someone to have fun with, for someone to do things with? How lucky they are to have that. I wish I had that too. I would be so happy, and I would enjoy making them happy too.

Suddenly, the lump in her throat grew several inches bigger! As it did, the feelings she was trying to hide were quickly bursting out of her skin.

Just then, a tear escaped her eyelid and rolled down her cheek. Before she could allow anything else to happen, she left the table undetected and unnoticed, in an awful rush. There was a fear and panic that crippled her, when she could no longer control the false face she was wearing.

In a busy, chaotic and noisy house, the little girl looked for an empty room in desperation, a room where she could be herself, cry and set her body free. She needed peace to think, a space she could let it all out, without fear or worry. It would be a room where she could breathe and relax, spending valuable time with her thoughts to analyse her situation. A space where she could take off the heavy mask she was wearing, if only for a break. It would be a huge relief for a little girl who never thought she could fit in with the family she was born into. Hers was a voice that was unheard and unspoken, one less important than the others, and her feelings only enhanced her one wish; the need for someone just for her, for company.

As the little girl found an empty room, she sat down on a comfortable seat. Her feet feeling lighter and at ease, as the weight of her shoulders sunk her into the soft and cosy, red velvet chair. The quiet air sang to her notes of peace, as she could finally transform back into herself, to feel what she wanted to feel, in that moment. She could still hear the laughter faded in the background, and with that the tears came rolling down her face, one after another.

Her emotions seemed to flow like a river, with no means of stopping. Sniffling and deep breaths took over her, as she could finally let go of her pain.

It was the hurt that came from not having a friend, the sorrow that came from loneliness. Until, in an instant, she got an idea! With that, her face started to dry. A solution had arrived, as she smiled at the baby Jesus in a manger, the nativity scene that lit up the whole room, the miracle that was Christmas. *I should say a prayer,* the little girl thought, as she looked at the baby Jesus so peacefully asleep in his crib.

"Well Jesus, you came on Christmas Day to be with us, if a prayer won't work today, it never will."

The little girl started rubbing the tears from her eyes with much determination, but before she continued her Christmas prayer, she took a much-needed deep breath, as her lack of energy and extreme upset were fast becoming a struggle.

"Jesus, I love you, but I need something from you. Someone! A special friend! I need the love and happiness that would come from a soulmate, someone to care for, and who loves me just as much as I would love them. Please help me, Jesus. I don't want to be alone any more! I know you will help me! I just have to be patient, and you will hear my Christmas prayer."

As the little girl smiled at the baby Jesus once more, she finished her prayer and got up from her knees.

While she composed herself to go back into reality again, she realised the lump in her throat had gone. She felt free, no longer choked up about anyone or anything!

As she was leaving the room, she looked back at the nativity scene with a smile that lifted her lips, a facial expression that could only be explained by the most endearing thought. *Sometimes, when you are feeling down, a good cry can sort it all out, and crying and talking to you has definitely helped me.*

And, as the little girl wished the baby Jesus a happy birthday, she left the room more content and happy.

A few years had passed by, and that little girl was not so little any more. She was a grown-up, a dedicated writer, with nothing on her mind other than the characters she had made for her books. She loved writing stories for little kids to make them laugh, funny and amazing stories. But that Christmas prayer, she had said when she was a little girl, had long been forgotten, as was her wish.

Until…

…on a train into town, the woman sat all by herself, deep in concentration, reading, writing, and reading again. Nothing around her existed! Nothing around her mattered, other than the characters she was making. She was a woman who enjoyed creating her own happy endings, whenever she liked. She created a place where loneliness did not exist, a place she could invent for others to enjoy too.

To her, she was all alone, as she sat deep in thought aboard a fast-moving train, but she was not on her own at all! Not really.

A handsome stranger, who had been watching her work from afar, could not help but admire how pretty she was. He was a businessman with his own busy schedule and who had his own work to do, but every time he went to concentrate, he was distracted, completely thrown by the beautiful woman sitting in his view with her golden hair and deep brown eyes. He had never seen anyone so radiant, so independent and carefree. He could not help but stare at her with admiration, although touched by a love bug, it made him look like a goof. Suddenly, before anybody noticed his creepiness, he snapped out of his staring – whilst a thought came to his mind.

How could I like someone I barely know? Pull

yourself together man! the handsome stranger thought, scolding himself, whilst trying to get back to his work.

He could barely put pen to paper, as he looked at her again. Suddenly, out of the blue, the handsome stranger developed his own wish – a wish he hoped would come true more than anything else in the world!

He needed to know the pretty woman. He wished he could be a part of her life, to be with her. He could only watch as his heart for her grew and grew. With that, back into his thoughts he drifted.

Should I go up to her? How can I go up and talk to her? She is completely out of my league! And what if I do talk to her and she knocks me back – what do I say then? the man thought, quietly agonising about what to do and fretting about the what-ifs.

All at once, the most stunning and gorgeous white feather drifted through an open window, a tilted window above the handsome stranger's head. Although the incoming wind moved the strands of his hair from side to side, he took no notice, his attention elsewhere!

As the big, white feather wafted through the air, it finally settled upon one of her books. The breathtaking scene escaping their notice, as they were both stuck in their heads.

The open window swept the chill in, like a Hoover picks up dust. The cold air reached the pretty, oblivious woman, as she sat so quietly with her books. Immediately, without thought, she stopped! She could feel it without looking up, without searching for what was causing her to instantly shiver. She opened her bag and took out her pink, knitted cardigan, putting it on, not taking her eyes off her work as she did.

While slipping into it, she caught his stare and smiled at him. It was a smile that encouraged his inner being to fall for her more and more, a smile he would forever remember, forever think about.

This girl is special! Different.

Ten minutes had passed by, and the woman was still cold. The cardigan she had pulled on clearly was not working, as the woman started to shiver excessively. It did not matter how tightly she wrapped herself up in it, she could feel the freezing air touching her skin, washing it with cruelty. She was not escaping it even though she had desperately tried!

She finally looked up and saw the open window above the handsome stranger. His dark hair and bright blue eyes captured her attention, and the woman was suddenly distracted. It was a rare moment for someone who had only one passion in life – to write, to create her own happy endings for children, for a little girl that used to be her.

The woman desperately wanted to ask the stranger to close his window, but she struggled. She did not want to annoy the man, dressed in a suit and who was occasionally smiling at her. She did not want to sound too bossy, or too demanding.

The woman sat there freezing in her skin, whilst her body started to complain; a silent agony, a frustration with herself.

She never had the courage to talk to people. She always wanted to say things that were in her head, but she never could. When she could not say what she wanted to, she would be so annoyed with herself. She would feel so restricted. No matter how hard she tried, her body would not let her do it, to speak for herself, to be her. Always thinking, *I am not important enough, I am too much of a bother, I am only a complainer; pathetic!* She had all these negative feelings which stopped her from being, well, her.

The chill had reached its maximum point when the woman could not cope any more, shivering uncontrollably. As she looked up at the handsome stranger, she caught his stare again. His own infatuation with her, bounced straight off her. She was totally clueless. She was a smart girl but not when it came to relationships. Her level of smart was as much as a banana.

"Sorry, excuse me sir," the woman started, taking encouragement from somewhere unbeknown. Her voice was a little shaky as she began to speak, although perhaps the hairs now standing up on her arms and body played their own part with her sudden outburst of confidence, her sudden release of inner strength.

"Yes?" asked the overenthusiastic stranger. His polite and bubbly personality, not to mention his good looks, became the complete picture in her eyes. She was not expecting it. She did not see it coming – how much she liked him! How much she was taken in by him. Yet, she would never, ever have admitted it. She found it difficult to ask a man to close a window, never mind anything else.

"Would you mind, if it's not too much trouble, to close your window?" the woman asked. "It's just, I wouldn't ask, but I am freezing," explained the woman.

The handsome stranger was surprised; he had never expected her to speak to him at all. He looked at her in amazement. She had such a warm, soothing, and welcoming voice, and as soon as she had finished speaking, he jumped up from his seat, as though he had a sudden urge to pee. He moved with energy to please her.

"Yes! Certainly. No problem. A woman like you

should not be freezing in this weather," said the man, blushing clearly, and stumbling over his words a little, as he shut the window that bothered her.

"Thank you so much! You are very kind!" said the woman, who was delighted she did not have to endure the cold any longer.

As they looked at each other a little awkwardly, struggling to find some words, the woman was keen to get back to her book, the only world that was not confusing to her in that moment. As she gave him one last smile, she lifted her book and continued where she had left off.

Still, it was no good. She was thinking of the handsome stranger. She was reading but nothing was going in.

What has he done to me? she thought. *Although, he's so nice, and good-looking too! I better not look up in case he's looking at me,* she continued, silently talking to herself.

The woman could not help it, as she struggled to think about anything else. Her mind had been captured. She looked up, hoping to get a glimpse of him without him noticing, and there it was, she met his stare again. Rather nervously, she quickly looked away, pretending to go back to her book.

The handsome stranger was smitten. They were both shy, but he was encouraged! His enthusiasm was growing for the perfect woman, for her. Taking matters and his feelings into his own hands, he got up from his seat, enticed to go and speak to the wonderful lady. Instantly, everybody looked up at him, and he quickly sat back down again with grave anxiety.

No, I can't! he thought, too frightened to speak with the pretty woman, terrified of all the staring and forceful eyes set upon him.

Finally, after several minutes of breathing exercises, he wiped the sweat away from his face and decided to give it another go. He walked up to the woman who was *deep* into her book, the woman he had to know, the woman who was not really reading her book at all.

Suddenly, as he stood beside her seat, she froze

like a stunned deer, stuck! She had NO clue what to do, the banana side of her brain coming back to play with her again, though to the handsome stranger, she simply had not seen him yet. To him, he was nothing in comparison to her, so he stood there like a statue, with no words coming from his lips, but all the while expecting her eyes to meet his.

The woman could not do anything as he stood beside her, still frozen and agitated with fear herself. Then it happened! The handsome stranger plucked up the courage to get her attention. He had the perfect plan, a clever idea. He was going to be brave and make the first move.

He coughed!

She looked up at him and smiled. It was the smile he loved so much, the smile that also, suddenly, had made him so anxious and jumpy.

"Can I sit with you?" the stranger asked, having rehearsed what he was going to say so many times before. The woman smiled at him again, hesitating before searching for words.

"Sure, I'd love that," scrambled the woman, giving the handsome stranger the confidence he had needed to talk to this beautiful lady with ease. It created a pleasant atmosphere that would slow down his heart rate, reduce his sweaty palms and his wet forehead.

"You know, this whole trip, I was hoping to get your attention!" said the man, making the woman nervously chuckle, as he began to complement her.

"Really?" she asked all surprised.

"Oh yes!" nodded the stranger with much enthusiasm and commitment for her. "My name is Luke, by the way," continued the nervous man.

"Please to meet you, Luke. My name is Jane," smiled the woman, a little nervous herself, as she shook his waiting hand.

Luke and Jane talked for several hours; time had escaped their attention. It had stood still while they were totally mesmerised by each other. The only thing that mattered to them were the eyes they were looking into, the hands that they were holding, the person they were enjoying talking to, and the possible future they would have together.

When the train stopped, their curiosity and joining souls could not depart, as they smiled at each other with contentment, sealing their approval.

"Want to go for something to eat?" asked a keen Luke.

"I'd love that!" smiled Jane, her curiosity to get to know him suddenly growing faster.

As they walked down a beautiful, cobbled street, the white feather appeared again behind them. Brushed delicately by the wind, this time it did not settle, continuing its journey somewhere unbeknown; an instrumental feather, its deeds unspoken, but working where words did not matter. It danced in the air, like it had a purpose, almost like its purpose was complete.

Suddenly, Luke had a thought that made him laugh, as they walked side by side to the nearest café.

"What?" asked Jane curiously, chuckling to herself.

"You know, whilst we were on that train, I wished

for you," said Luke.

"What!" chuckled an exhilarated Jane.

"Yeah," confirmed Luke, nodding his head slightly, before he continued. "On the train when I had seen you. I wished I could get to know you, become your friend."

Jane stopped on the spot, a little shocked, as he continued to speak. She could remember a moment in her life, something she was reliving as she shut her eyes, the white feather still floating in the air above their heads, as she did. Jane opened her eyes again and cleared her throat, before confessing to her new friend.

"That's so funny," laughed Jane, as she finally remembered the Christmas prayer she had said so many years ago as a little girl, "because I prayed for you."

THE END

When the beauty of your soul thinks to say a little prayer, and when the stress of this world forces you to forget all about it, God does not forget and your little prayer will live on. It will live on to surprise you someday, in the most unsuspecting of ways.

Hope is nothing without trying.

To try at anything is nothing without hope.

Hold onto them both as you climb life's ladder.

Do not let the stresses of this world pull you down!

Keep on climbing until you reach the top.

It's okay if you fall,

As we all do at some point or other.

What matters the most is that you can get back up.

Even if you must do it again and again and again!

Do not become discouraged,

As the best things come with trial and perseverance.

Do not live your life by everybody else's standards,

Live it for you — the person that matters!

Count your blessings and let your heart be glad,

As loneliness is a feeling that will never be forever!

www.ingramcontent.com/pod-product-compliance
Lightning Source LLC
Chambersburg PA
CBHW032135050726
47590CB00008B/3103